Dog Sc

I have a dog
named Fergus.

When I say SIT,
Fergus jumps up.

When I say STAY,
Fergus runs away.

When I say COME,
Fergus wants to play!

2

I am taking Fergus
to dog school.

There are lots of dogs
at dog school.

Some dogs are big,
and some dogs are small.
Some dogs are hairy,
and some dogs are scary!

All the dogs at dog school
learn how to sit.

Now when I say SIT,
Fergus sits.

I tell Fergus
that he is a good dog.
Then we play.

All the dogs at dog school
learn how to stay.

Now when I say STAY,
Fergus stays.

I tell Fergus
that he is a good dog.
Then we play.

All the dogs at dog school learn how to come.

Sometimes
when I say COME,
Fergus comes.

Most of the time
when I say COME,
Fergus still wants to play!

Fergus and I are learning
other things at dog school.

When I say HEEL,
Fergus stays by my side.

When I say DOWN,
Fergus lies down.

When I say SHAKE,
Fergus gives me his paw!

Fergus and I had fun
at dog school.

I learned
how to give
Fergus commands.

Fergus learned
how to obey me
so that he can be safe.

But, best of all,
Fergus and I
made new friends
at dog school.